BLACK SUN KINTSUGI

Veins of Light in Darkest Night

RAGHAV MURALI

INDIA • SINGAPORE • MALAYSIA

ISBN
Paperback 979-8-89673-438-3
Hardcase 979-8-89699-304-9

"There is a crack in everything, that's how the light gets in."
- Leonard Cohen, 'Anthem', 1992

"Poetry is in the observation"
- Arvind Dev, 2023

"Every once in a while, you gotta take that L for the art"
- Smriti Murali, 2023

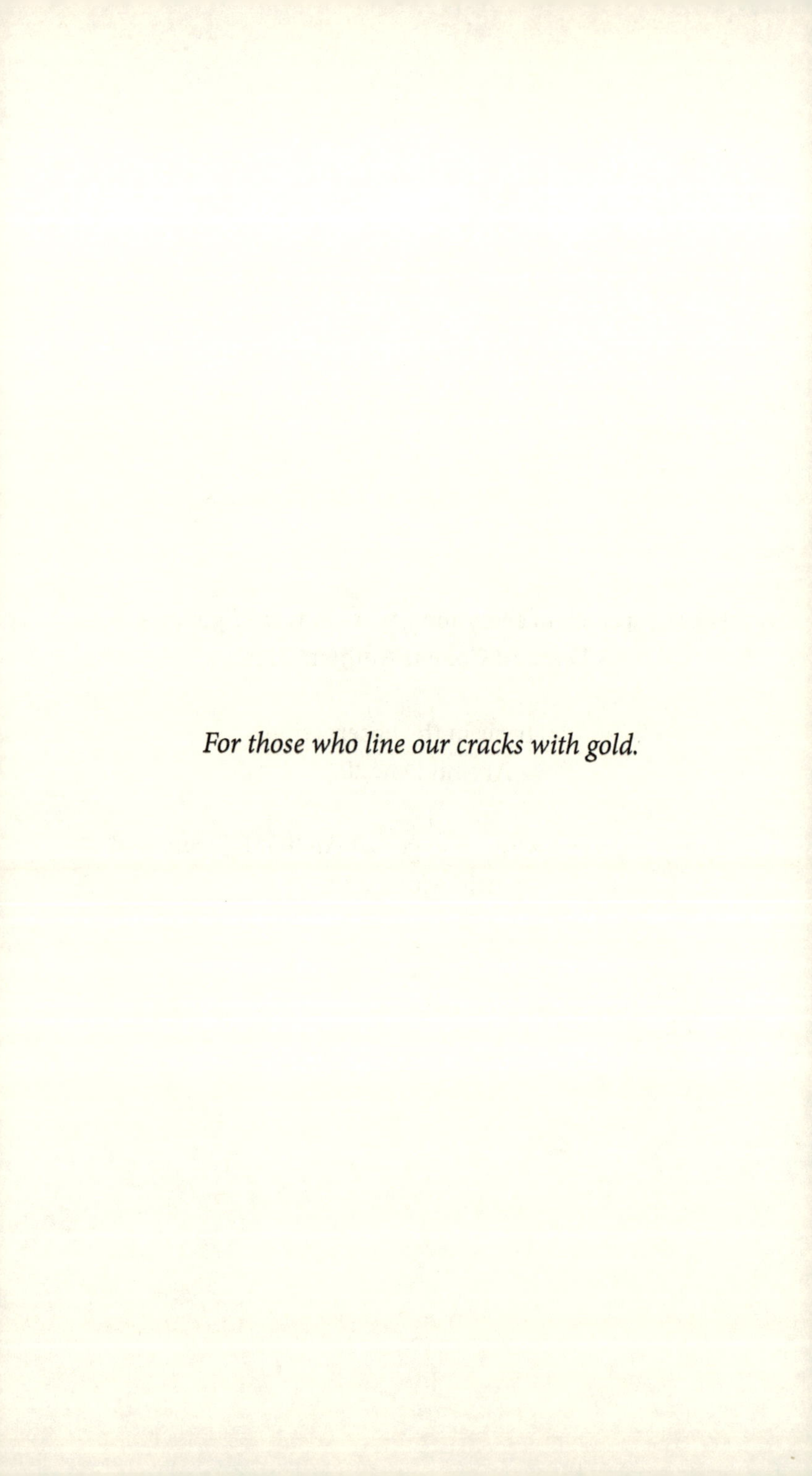

For those who line our cracks with gold.

CONTENTS

II. Heartbroken Robots

III. Liquid Dreams, Subconscious Streams

IV. Human Nature

V. Dawn

PRELUDE

Our lives are an emulsion of events and decisions, painting pathways, layering the bricks upon the crossroads of destiny. The words contained in this book were formed from reflections of such occasions and the fleeting moments of clarity that I have faced at these junctures.
Many of the pieces contained within these pages were formed during periods of struggle, and they accordingly reflect as much. However, the formation of this outlet has in turn lightened the load upon the self and enabled this release into the world.

This book is split into five sections. The first explores the cyclical nature of life and death. The second explores romance and associated failures. The third, as its name suggests, explores the transient nature of reality. The fourth are reflections on humanity and nature. The final section, 'Dawn', reflects in moments, a journey across a year, across events, across a varied set of emotions. A journey from the darkness within, in search of the light.

What does the title of this book "Black Sun Kintsugi" mean?

A "Black Sun" is like the words suggest, a solar eclipse. An obscuring of the sun's light on earth by the celestial happenstance of the moon's orbit. Perhaps an apt representation of the paths we take to destinies unknown. The mysteries of life, hidden. The source of life and wonder itself, concealed. Sometimes, simply, the inability to see the light beyond the darkness.

Kintsugi is the ancient Japanese art of repairing broken pottery by mending the areas of breakage with powdered gold. A means of embracing the imperfections that make up our personal histories. The cracks of light that seep through overwhelming tenebrosity. Hope perhaps?

A friend once said to me, "what do we have, if not hope?". Let that remain with you beyond this reading, along with my love and gratitude for you.

I

ENDLESS BEGINNINGS

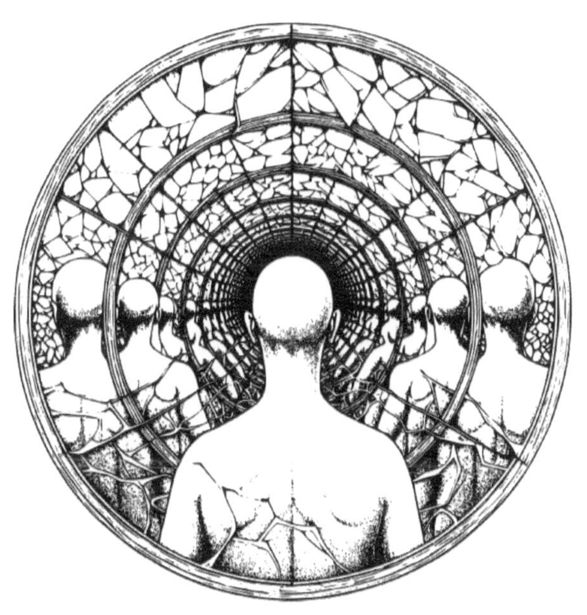

Life and death,
each other beget.

Art is born
often, from intent.
Sometimes, however,
it is birthed by circumstance.
Moments of inspiration conceived
through uncommon misconceptions
discarded by daily innate circumspection.

What is art
if not the
spectacular
vernacular
of the spirit?

Think outside the box, they say.
But what if
there is no box?

Either you make time
Or time makes you.

Our constant rebirths
find their graves
in our own words.

In my darkness,
once resided a terrible beast,
perpetually unquenched,
raging, perplexed.

Now, the same darkness
has become a shelter
for feelings unacknowledged,
and expectations unmet.

Until, that is, light
shines its face upon it.

FALL

The fall is often pitted
against the rise,
shamed, negated.

But what if you are the rain?
Then fall you must
so life can rise from your waters.

In the perpetuity of seasons
the beauty of autumn leaves
commands attention
before winter's drought
paves pathways for
the flowers of spring.

One who has lost everything
can no longer a loser be,
for now they have everything to gain.

GANG

Nature, at her merciless, horrific finest,
beckoned me witness,
her fierce indifference.

Half a dozen dogs
ripped the now lifeless,
mangled body, apart.

The cat I presume had been
caught unawares, or perhaps
it picked the fight.

Assumed the upper hand,
but did not foresee,
the pack lurking nearby.

The commotion drew me there,
but by the time I had located it,
the cries of retaliation had been subdued.

The pack lost interest shortly after,
each member leaving
with a souvenir.

The last to leave dragged the victim away,
ensuring no evidence was left behind.
Only the silent aftermath remained.

Where is docked the boat
upon which thou needst float
when the rapids they coerce
currents to face thee averse.

Kindness and sorrow,
hand in hand, imprisoned,
bound by each other.

Their hold cannot relinquish,
for if one were to be alone,
it may never itself be seen.

The grief you carry weighs upon the rest of us.

Death and destiny,
both tails of tales,
innate fodder for
saplings to emerge
as threads of a yarn
yet to be spun.

GABE

You, seeker of truths
went exploring one day
but someone chose
to take your life away.

It takes only one bullet
but you were gifted seven.
I can only hope that
you felt none of them.

Sadly there will be
no answers found.
So many questions
reeling unwound.

Those who did this,
if only they knew,
you could have lit
up their lives too.

Such is the nature of flow.
It is inherently directional.
Like time, and rivers.

DREAD

Sometimes you dream of the dead.
Sometimes you want to.

Sometimes you need
the dream to feel connected
because someone else
might be more spiritual than you

But sometimes the dreams
are filled with dread
because sometimes, the dead
they dream of you.

There is beauty in death
like ice on the precipice of melting
we see through to the other side
as it holds on to its waning solidity
clear as the state it will soon be.

ASHES

The dead are never
truly gone until
all whom ever knew,
loved, or remembered them
cease to remain.

Some traverse lifetimes
in photographs, paintings,
or an etch on a tree.
Existing in theory, until
the artefact meets its demise.

They may, on occasion, return
in dreams and memories,
of those whose DNA
hold the imprints
of their existence.

Ashes of lifetimes past,
scattered by winds of change.
Stains of love upon
a twig of destiny, splintered,
from the tree of life.

II

HEARTBROKEN ROBOTS

In the land of dreams and promises,
hope is the thread woven
into the fabric of pursuit.

And I am once again he
who lunges into traps of old.
Gold in the game of dice
between dreams and hope.

COMMUTE

I saw the moon
full and bright,
so I sent her to you.

Then I learned
the moon represents
forbidden love
in our subcontinent.

Later,
I saw an old couple
sharing headphones
on the train.

LIPS

In the mirror his attention grips
the sight of his rarely used lips.

Our lips become more kissable
the more we let them kiss.

We reminisce of unmatched bliss
found in her whispers' hiss.

Upon his reflection, his eyes slip
to notice his disappearing lips.

If love it stays too long amiss,
there may be no lips left to kiss.

JUDGEMENTS OF LONELY MEN

She shows
herself.
More.
Cute pics
and all
is not well
at home.

Solitude can be a choice,
but loneliness is always
an unchosen companion.

Solitude,
the companion you choose,
But tis loneliness
that chooses you.

Sometimes,
Loneliness chooses
your companion
for you.

My heart
has been stolen
so many times,
I wonder often
if it is still
the same heart
or if I've grown
new hearts
many times over.

We have a tendency
to give our heart away
to those who don't view us
in the same light as we view them.
We then wander the earth,
meeting other wonderful people,
for whom we have no heart left to give.

THE HEART TREE

His heart was broken,
so the pieces he buried.
In their place, a tree grew.

Its branches held fruits.
Lesser hearts, pumping
love, in seeming infinitude.

He could now give his heart
to countless others too.
The more he gave away,
the more hearts grew.

But the seemingly infinite,
almost wearily withdrew.
Until he realized,
love was the fertilizer too.

The subtle art of self loathing
is like warm winter clothing,
layered against the freezing chill
from winds of hope atop a hill.

The sun, it seems
heard my lament
that she had kissed you,
so she kissed me too
and warmed my cold heart.

Travesty it looms in delight
knowing fully well that despite
all your efforts to be precise
you will never truly be right.

Time heals some wounds,
but what happens
to those time forgets?

In the intermittence
when we reach to the sky
with a cry for help,
tis often, not the aid we seek,
but an ear, for our lamentations.

"You're living in a bubble," she said.
I'm sure I do.
But I didn't want to tell her,
"So are you".

When you stared at me,
was it perhaps a monster
you hoped to see?

What faced you instead,
was a capacity for love so great,
it was far more terrifying
than any monster could be.

HEARTBREAKER

I was elated
that somehow
my reaching out
had moved you.

Instead, I uncovered
in full blown clarity
that robots can be
heartbreakers too.

A privilege
of endless pain
is the potential
for endless creation.

GRIEF

Grief is often found
seated in realities past.
We tend to mourn loss
of things, people, love.

Lately, I have discovered
a novel, peculiar grief.
One that enables me lament
realities not experienced.

It resides in time non-existent.
Outside future, present, and past.
The post-partum of rejection,
a creation of dejection.

How does one return
to the here and now
when no doors exist
in the realm of sorrow.

The heart desires
amorous canoodles
but the only oodle
the gut guzzles
are salty late night
instant noodles.

ACCEPTANCE

I once described
meaning as an ocean tide,
but tis acceptance
which looks back at me.

Like the dance of a slinky
my hopes beckon reality
as if their back and forth
will magically bequeath
my desires upon thee.

Though meaning it may
wash over unexpectedly,
only time cascades
down the staircase
until acceptance hits me
square in the face.

Under the street lamp he waited
as she crossed the beam of light.
Unaware as I witnessed them,
one jet black, the other snow white.
Entwined as the moon and darkness,
the two cats ventured into the night.
Our paths crossed as the city slept,
apathetic to the lovers' delight.

III

LIQUID DREAMS, SUBCONSCIOUS STREAMS

Water takes shape.
Wind creates it.

Stories transcend
where the line blurs
between reality and fiction.

ITHICUS PITHICUS

Ithicus pithicus
a creature so mythicus
seemed ape from afar
till it took a good look at us.

Gleaming in the reflection
of the undersea moon
among the coral trees
where neon flowers bloom.

One eye or twenty?
A bulbous affair,
missing nothing
it sees aplenty.

Seemingly in perennial slumber
a blink lasts days
so the onlooker sees
only a moment in eternity.

So vast in form is it,
Earth has grown over
where it apparently sits
in wait for its lost lover.

In the camouflaged gloom
one might swim right past
as it picks its teeth
with sunken ships' masts.

How pitiful to witness it,
the forlorn, enduring Ithicus,
who took refuge in the depths
because he once pitied us.

My heart, it sinks deep, heavy.
Wretched cogitations they scheme.
Friends I miss but cannot meet,
seeds of love, which would not be,
debts from which I get no relief.
Merciless, they churn, like wheels,
reveries of self-induced misery.
Sleep in all its forms eludes me.

GLIMPSES OF THE NIGHT

A city comatose, suspires beneath a clear, starlit sky, warmed by a moth-eaten blanket of street lamps.

* * *

The shell of a fallen egg, shattered, faintly scattered. Sheltered in between, the yolk, perfectly intact, a midnight sun, greets me, proud of its achievement. Will it last the night? Seems unlikely. Peckish scavengers lurk nearby.

* * *

A lackadaisical breeze gently tumbles through the streets, dandruffed with pollution dust. Empty, except for a few loners like myself, who dot the scape.

The zephyr ignites a whiff of lost memories. Observations of lanes that once held fog, and condensed sighs of mystic trees. Now, parked vehicles outnumber the weary branches and browned leaves of the handful that remain.

Arbitrary pyres emit plastic smoke, rotten ashes of a city prematurely aged, decomposing, consumed by a bacterial humanity. Dreams of a society plentiful, thriving, like a carcass, float in the ether.

* * *

A sight for sore eyes, a young barely-man and his furry companion stroll by leashless. It is evident, the love shared between them is enough to hold them together.

The canine radiates wisdom in abundance, revealed perhaps by the limp in his gait. It overshadows his otherwise diminutive stature. It's unclear who has seen more winters, for the dog seems the guide, and the boy his apprentice.

Are we the introspection of the universe
or the extrospection of our cells?

PIZZERIA

In this dream,
I had a kitten named Naru.

A didi had come to clean.
I had left the stove on it seems,
but somehow nothing had burned.

Where had I been?
Spying on some friends
who had invited me
to join them that evening.
It was a pizzeria.

The room in which I hid,
stored some freshly baked pizzas
in large oven like cupboards.
They seemed ready to be delivered,
warm in their boxes.

My greed got the better of me.
I opened a box and stole
a couple of toppings.
It was fresh and delicious.
Were they tomatoes?
I couldn't tell,
but they were crunchy.

I shortly departed out the back,
hooded, in the drizzle.
Back to my apartment,
where Naru waited inside,
and the didi waited outside,
for me.

If truth and pain both hurt,
perhaps, sometimes,
they are the same.

At times when the mind seeks emptiness,
is often when emptiness eludes the mind.
The heart says, two can play that game.

LINGER

The allure of what could be
is often so strong
it overpowers reality.

A momentary glimpse
can leave an impression
decades long,
while a life lived
can be forgotten
in almost an instant.

What can be,
can get lost
when the could be
lingers beyond its welcome.

PEACE

To think
or not to think
is almost never the question.
Tis simply
a state of being
thrust upon the self.
A plethora
of imagined choices,
designed seemingly
with the sole purpose
of keeping peace at bay.

The subconscious leaks
into the world of the awake
through the scars, porous,
despite the respite
the body seeks,
from the drainage
the day left in its wake.

THE HORSE

A late weekday afternoon it was,
as we sipped tea under a parasol.
It felt a day like any other,
but we were interrupted by
a sight uncommon in these parts.

A rickety old man sat
upon a rickety old cart,
helmed by a rickety old horse.
Together, they were
an understated deadpan vision
of time hence passed.

He enquired of us directions
to a nearby destination.
We had to ask him
some of our own questions
to understand how best to aid him.

It was the man
to whom we gave the directions,
but it was the horse
who moved on his own accord,
as if he understood our words.

The man seemed
to barely understand
a word of what we said,
but somehow
the horse knew
exactly what to do,
and the trust between them
was such that
the man literally did nothing.

And just as they had appeared,
in a moment,
they were gone.

DELIGHT

Delight is a word
best described
through experience.

Behold, my mother at the beach.
She cannot swim,
but that does not taper
her unbridled child-like joy
while she splashes around
knee deep, in the surf,
holding my father's hand,
his stoic joy in admiring hers.

Elsewhere, my niece, a toddler,
dons her flowery sunglasses.
The teeny tiny don trots around
beaming from ear to ear.

Perhaps much of the weight
we carry around with us,
could be significantly lightened,
if we could simply rejoice
in the delight of others,
those around us,
and our loved ones.

VALIDATION

Why do we feel
the need
to talk about ourselves?
To express our selves.
All of us.

When we don't,
we feel lost,
unheard,
unimportant,
invalidated.

Is our expression
only for validation?
All of us?

Perhaps, we are,
all of us, simply,
the expressions,
the validation
for this universe,
and it in turn
for the greater beyond.

A perpetual infinitude
of validating existence.
Inward and outward.

I am here.
I exist.

And that's all she wrote.

On the precipice.
Reality unwinds.
Dreams snatched away.

How shall we bereave
elements lost in between
all that our dreams weave.

Sorry it had to be this way.
I tend to eat my feelings away.

When seeking
the right words
to express
I often run
out of them.

LABYRINTHS

The thing with labyrinths
is, at times
they can be
deceivingly small.

One such place
is a tiny bookstore
I sometimes frequent.

In entirety
it is barely
the size of
a single occupant bedroom,
but I have spent hours there –
not all at once,
as in the traditional sense
of spending hours at a time
at any given place –
but perusing
for extended stretches
of minute ages flown by,

losing myself
to the limited,
but diverse
and intriguing titles,
which line the shelves.

A labyrinth which
I often tend to leave
with more than I entered.

PRIMORDIAL

Ancient is the wolf,
an old soul he be.
His self unearths,
forgotten histories.

A child of the land,
he braves the seas,
till at last he reaches
a volcanic destiny.

Upon his weary frame
its flames unleash.
Completely engulfed
as the sun is he.

Forged in the inferno
a dragon he becomes.
A primordial entity,
equal to none.

IV

HUMAN NATURE

Society and I
don't always see
eye to eye.

GAZE

I won't apologize
for finding my gaze
upon your
distant elegance
while you strutted
distracted
perhaps flustered,
shifting your things
in your subconscious
search for homeostasis.

I will apologize
for the discomfort
you felt when
your senses tingled
upon feeling my gaze.
Moments had to pass
before I uncovered
my passive admiration
caused you
undue distress.

Who knows how many
innocent admirers
have fostered fear,
disgust in deterrence,
unintentionally,
unwittingly,
while only
wanting to embrace
in the moment,
a beautiful observation.

When nothing is said by opinions voiced,
silence is the optimal weapon of choice.

But if injustice witnessed dare escape,
silence becomes violence in shame.

Roots,
tethers,
leashes.
All hold on
to something, yet
serve different masters.

The leash restrains,
imprisons the beast.

A tether protects
the boat from floating adrift,
but must be released
if the vessel intends to sail.

But roots, they spread
so the tree can grow.

Cyclone asks the sea,
does our love intimidate?
Beaches might know best.

DEAD HEROES

These are the days
of dead heroes
systematically outed,
as villains concealed.

Devious connivers
who deceived us
for their misguided gains,
in benefit of the few.

Or simply, wealthy buffoons
who wronged us
with their incompetence
and inherited arrogance.

Notoriously, flawed, human,
with lives slightly unordinary.
Surrounded by evangelists
holding golden pedestals.

The slightness, exponentially
magnified by time
and the memories
of those who followed.

There is only one rule.
There are no rules here.

The only rules that matter
are the ones we choose
for our selves to follow.

You address the room,
but we both know
the message is for me.

That thing
you hold on to
for dear life
is the very thing
that oppresses you.

GATEKEEPER

Who are you
to build these gates?
What right have you
to keep me
from exploring this earth
while you roam free.
The same earth from which
you and I both be.

This world is my birthright
same as yours.
Not to own it, but simply
to see it in its splendor.
To witness it breathe.
To lie on its surface
wherever I please.

To love it, and
be loved by it.

How many like me
have been denied,
love and fortune
we've left behind,
for physical distance
we have perceived
when we could simply
have crossed the seas,
instead to be met with
your gates lacquered
with the paint of your
self-anointed superiority.

I am a conundrum of humanity.
A creature born of this earth,
practitioner of imagined free will,
but held back indefinitely
by arbitrary notions of nationality.

Leave something
to the imagination
they said.
The imagined nation.
Is that not
all our nations?

STEEPED

We are the ones awoken
by insipid systems, broken,
well spoken, privileged
to have eyes wide open.

Yet, steeped chest deep
sleepless, we witness
boundless kindness lost,
fostered by pious blindness.

Unfulfilled expectations
drown erstwhile generations,
with predecessors entitled
to undue veneration.

There's always something to talk about,
and if there isn't,
silence is perfectly acceptable.

Where lies reason in times of tragedy?
Why does tragedy romance death so?
When questions beget only questions
can those left behind ever find solace?

BAGGAGE

This baggage
I find myself hauling
bears the weight
of blind adherence
to societal narratives
that span generations
spamming us everyday
with expectations
scamming our future,
invalidating deviations
from perceived norms
sculpted afore us.

Layer the flavor,
waste no taste,
they work not
when done in haste.

We often get lost
in narratives
formed by others
we sometimes forget
to pave our own.

VESSEL

In the hopes of owning all,
some inadvertently become a vessel.
One that holds the water,
which takes its shape.
Are they forever stuck?
For only the water can evaporate,
while the vessel must
bear the burden
of all the water it holds.

The vessel lightens its load
only when more water evaporates.
Oh, the irony.
The vessel continues
to create entrapments
to keep the water within,
perhaps unwittingly
overfilling itself
to the point of tipping over,
and all is lost.

You wouldn't know
personal space
if it licked you
in the face.

TEMPEST

You approach me
as a storm, assuming
a raging tempest
will quell the ship
that sails this sea.
But can you not see?
Your winds and rains
cannot infiltrate
my ocean depths.
I am stillness, undeterred.
A refuge, unrelenting,
for monsters unknown.
Purveyor of cycles,
preserver of life,
perseverance imbibed.
We aren't enemies,
your self and I,
for ships you must wreck
so my krakens can feed.
Your raging storm
will inevitably subside
but my dark depths
will sway the tides.

The fog of our love
exhales like smoke
from the twisted nail
upon dilapidated threads
of the barb wire fence
separating us both
while you reflect
across me here
on our balcony.

PROGRESS

Two steps forward, one step back
is the rhythm of progress.
This iteration seems reversed.

At rock bottom, the hard floor
was comforting to know
there was nowhere lower to go.

Now, a few steps ahead,
the step back has left
a bed to sleep in, sound.

But the feeling of sinking
digs slowly deeper into
lost caverns underground.

Sorrow
presents itself
as poetic expression.

Pretty words,
a genesis
of the desolate
despondency
bearing witness,
unable to act,
or be helpful.
A wretched situation.

Temporary consolation,
the woeful prize.

Such raconteurs we be
of narratives we fabricate
before actuality transpires
in the lives of others

SERENITY

Sometimes peace
requires intervention
other times,
simply observation.

Conversation brokers,
silence becomes,
while time can heal
or it can fester.

At times the justification
for violent eradication
reflects in the ineffectiveness
of peaceful protest.

Accepting the possibility
that peace may never be
might alone be the path
which leads to serenity.

One must remember
the world moves ahead
despite the losses
of lives untold
life goes on
stories unfold
and we feel entitled
to take ourselves
a bit too seriously.

GRAVITY

Gravity determines
all that rises will fall.
Ships that sink
swallowed up whole,
crushed into molten rock.

Yet, the same fields,
the eternal orbits
enable them to transform,
rise again as clouds,
shower the earth as rain,
replenishing, rejuvenating.

Nutrients for seedlings
that shall one day
grow into trees.
Providing shade and respite
for future generations.

While the sun is the giver of life,
some plants need shade to grow.

V. DAWN

Sunrise, the day's birth,
awake to reveal the sky
erupting with mirth.

Some days I read, some days I write.
Other days I feel my heart ignite.
The fire, it burns everything in sight.
Until only embers remain in the night.

THE CAVE

Atop a jebel cave of light,
a phoenix of the sun,
invited into her abode,
a wolf of the moon.

A hazy dessert of herbs
they shared under her roof,
as he stoically admired her,
but remained restrained, aloof.

Mired in pasts bygone
of preconceived notions' gloom.
amongst cloudy futures,
was this destined for doom?

Through these unanswerables construed,
alas, the present, it went amiss.
As he lay awake that night he rued,
that he did not give the phoenix a kiss.

A few months hence,
the wolf returned
to lands of the phoenix
and her high perch.

There was no light
or entry to the cave.
The mountain remained
a speck, far away.

Her candles burned
where he could not see
and her tattoos
remained a mystery.

Her decisions and convictions
were fortified by solitude.
The sun had set before it rose
like sand by ocean waves deposed.

I could feel
our hearts.
Beating.
Seeking.
Stealing.
Craving.
Escaping.
Stopping.
Slowing.
Saddening.
Beating.
A solemn drum.
Into the night.
Silent.

OF BIRDS AND WOLVES

If a bird and wolf
were together seek
to write a story yet untold,

Can the wolf grow wings,
or the bird shed hers,
to make earth and sky whole.

Shall it be that society
will cast them out to sea,
where neither has an abode.

Perhaps they can yet peruse,
while destiny lays in snooze,
what the future has in store.

Distance makes the heart grow fond,
but tis the same distance
which also cuts the string,
unties the knot that holds
the fondness firm.
Dries the well of hope,
which waters the seeds of love.

UNSAID

I thought of you today.

I actually think of you
more than I'd like to mention,
but to keep in terms with
the reality we live in,
where it might be
considered a parlance
of unhealthy obsessions,
to avoid incurring odium,
and the possibility
of your revulsion,
I curtail my own
attempts to reach out.

Hope you are keeping well.

Why can't we,
for just today,
ardent lovers be.
Though plainly,
painfully,
the end we both see.
Our boats they drift
unsubtly apart
as our separate quests
together seek
beyond the horizon,
a romance for eternity.

HYDROGEN

We are hydrogen
you and I.
Complete on our own.
Elemental, existential,
laden with immense potential.
Our combustion,
the sun can be.
Brightest of lights,
infinite intensity,
cradle of creation,
harbinger of creativity.
Helium, afloat in stability.
Even our end,
a supernova can be,
leaving behind nebulae
for all to see.

ITCH

And there it sat
next to a cup
empty, like a seat
and it looked
through the void
where a heart
once had been.

It moved on
a long time ago
yet it reminisced
of could haves
while bathing in
the endless itch
of should haves.

SPECK

Give enough time
or distance to another,
small it will appear.

Further still,
its minisculity might
feign invisibility.

Go far enough,
and all that remain
are questions and faith.

You might then wonder
if it was ever there
in the first place.

Despite the fact,
the now distant speck
in your heart, remains.

Ordinary feels
like leaves on a fallen tree.
A bird contemplates

To initiate
is to renegotiate
what already was.

A word unspoken,
a trail of thought now broken,
a mind awoken.

Exclusivity,
denies possibilities.
Love's potential lost.

Let us not resign
to limitations of our
inherent design.

You fight for your life
while we await your return.
This house lies vacant.

My presence
is my present
to you.

Wide-eyed wanderer,
where will you go tomorrow?
your time has ended.

As he fell asleep,
dawn broke upon the city.
A bird sang alone.

Remember, friend.
Our cosmic tango
with the sun and moon
dictates endless cycles
of new beginnings,
fresh starts, and rebirths.
While the onset of night
blankets us in darkness,
tis the only way to witness
light from the stars.
For nothing may be the end,
but it is also the place
where everything begins.
Always and forever.

CODA

I met a bug one morning. A beetle, presumedly lost. We crossed paths upon the landing of a staircase. I was going up, and he, well, I'm quite unsure.

"How did you get here?" I wondered. The entrance to the staircase was sealed by a door. He must have flown in when someone else had opened the door. Or perhaps he had come down here from another floor. Or perhaps, he's never been outdoors at all, and had lived his entire existence in the realm of the staircase of this building.

"How old are you?" I wondered. I'm no expert on insects, so when I was finally at my desk, some basic googling told me beetles' lifespans can range anywhere from 10 days for some species to 6 months for others. This fellow was on the larger side, so I presumed, perhaps he's one of the longer living variants of his kind.

In which case, I wondered, "have you lived your life's purpose?". It saddened me to think that perhaps this fellow had cut his own opportunities short by getting himself lost in this giant, sealed, staircase realm.

On the other hand, experience told me that this beetle had come here to die, after having accomplished his life's deed. I pondered upon the loneliness of his life. How he'd never pass on his story to anyone. No friends, no family, and even whoever he may have mated with, they would never see each other again.

Such privilege we have, that our lives are long enough to spend time with family, make friends, find love, experience loss, and face it all with a plethora of emotion and strength.

I felt sad for the beetle, but somehow in his lack of awareness, mine I acknowledged and cherished. For nothing remains forever, but blessed are we who have enough time to experience, reflect, and move on.

ACKNOWLEDGEMENTS

My sincerest gratitude to my family, friends, and the team at Notion Press. Thank you.

ABOUT THE AUTHOR

Raghav Murali is an entrepreneur, filmmaker, and educator based in Bangalore, India. His first poetry collection *The Temple of It* was released in April 2023. This is his second book.